THE HOBBYIST'S
BIOLOGY LAB NOTEBOOK

FOR HOME RESEARCH

Activinotes

Activinotes

DAILY JOURNALS, PLANNERS, NOTEBOOKS AND OTHER BLANK BOOKS

Copyright 2016

This Book Belongs To

_____

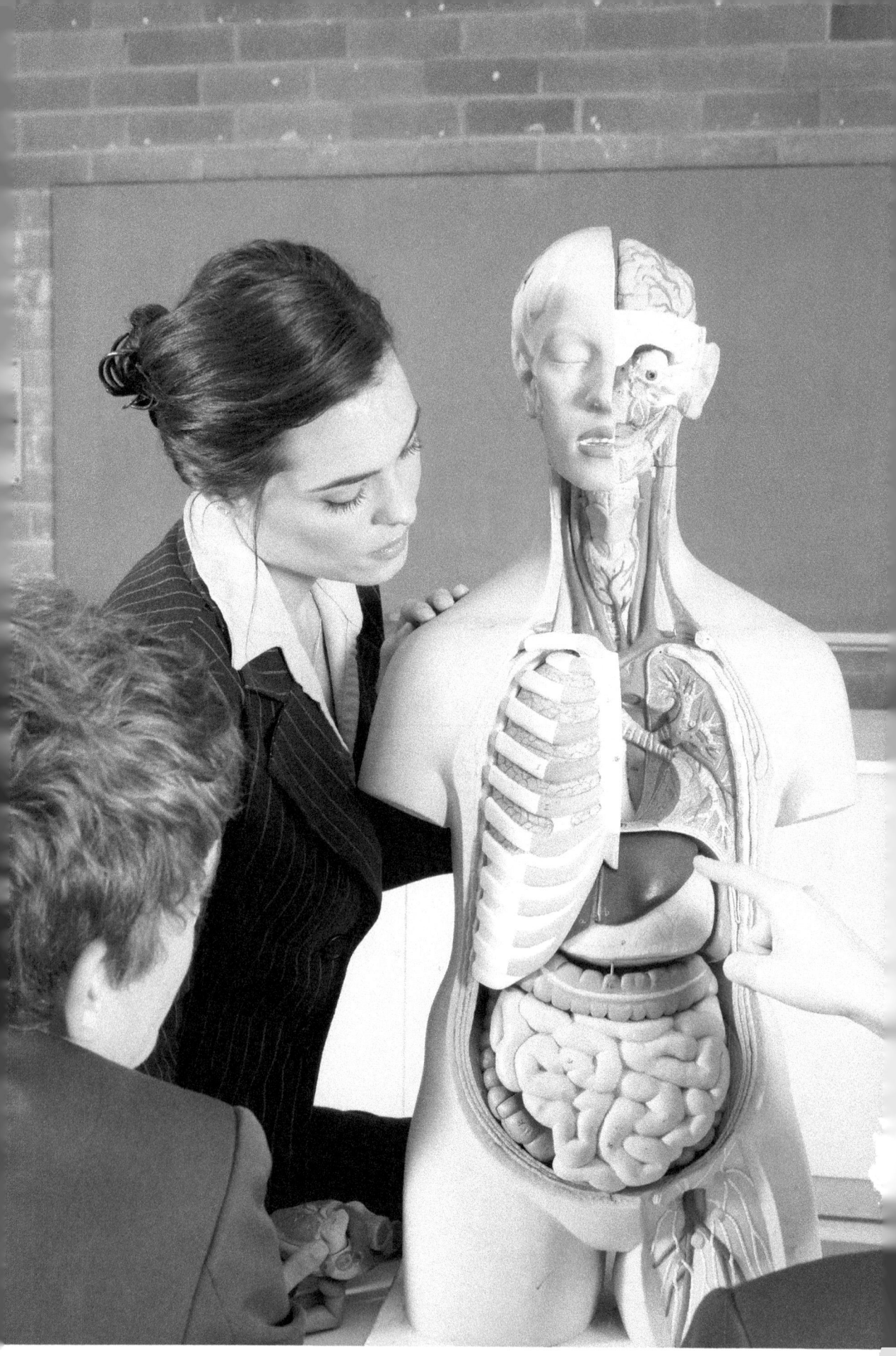

DATA

FIELD NAME	VALUE
Expiry date	
Sample Source	
Cell-Type	
Developmental Stage	
Medium	
Serum	
Percent	
Growth	
Temperature	
Doubling-Time	
Selectable Markers	
Propagation	

ANALYSIS

_____
_____
_____
_____
_____

CONCLUSION

_____
_____
_____
_____
_____

ANALYSIS

_____
_____
_____
_____
_____

CONCLUSION

_____
_____
_____
_____
_____
_____
_____
_____

DATA COLLECTION & PROCESSING

Levels/Marks	Aspect 1	Aspect 2	Aspect 3
	Recording Raw Data	Processing Raw Data	Presenting Raw Data

DATA

FIELD NAME	VALUE
Expiry date	
Sample Source	
Cell-Type	
Developmental Stage	
Medium	
Serum	
Percent	
Growth	
Temperature	
Doubling-Time	
Selectable Markers	
Propagation	

ANALYSIS

_____
_____
_____
_____
_____

CONCLUSION

_____
_____
_____
_____
_____

ANALYSIS

_____
_____
_____
_____
_____

CONCLUSION

_____
_____
_____
_____
_____
_____
_____
_____
_____

DATA COLLECTION & PROCESSING

Levels/Marks	Aspect 1	Aspect 2	Aspect 3
	Recording Raw Data	Processing Raw Data	Presenting Raw Data

DATA

FIELD NAME	VALUE
Expiry date	
Sample Source	
Cell-Type	
Developmental Stage	
Medium	
Serum	
Percent	
Growth	
Temperature	
Doubling-Time	
Selectable Markers	
Propagation	

ANALYSIS

_____
_____
_____
_____
_____

CONCLUSION

_____
_____
_____
_____
_____

ANALYSIS

_____
_____
_____
_____
_____

CONCLUSION

_____
_____
_____
_____
_____
_____
_____

DATA COLLECTION & PROCESSING

Levels/Marks	Aspect 1	Aspect 2	Aspect 3
	Recording Raw Data	Processing Raw Data	Presenting Raw Data

DATA	
FIELD NAME	VALUE
Expiry date	
Sample Source	
Cell-Type	
Developmental Stage	
Medium	
Serum	
Percent	
Growth	
Temperature	
Doubling-Time	
Selectable Markers	
Propagation	

ANALYSIS

_____
_____
_____
_____
_____

CONCLUSION

_____
_____
_____
_____
_____

ANALYSIS

_____
_____
_____
_____
_____

CONCLUSION

_____
_____
_____
_____
_____
_____
_____
_____

DATA COLLECTION & PROCESSING

Levels/Marks	Aspect 1	Aspect 2	Aspect 3
	Recording Raw Data	Processing Raw Data	Presenting Raw Data

DATA	
FIELD NAME	VALUE
Expiry date	
Sample Source	
Cell-Type	
Developmental Stage	
Medium	
Serum	
Percent	
Growth	
Temperature	
Doubling-Time	
Selectable Markers	
Propagation	

ANALYSIS

_____
_____
_____
_____
_____

CONCLUSION

_____
_____
_____
_____
_____

ANALYSIS

_____
_____
_____
_____
_____

CONCLUSION

_____
_____
_____
_____
_____
_____
_____

DATA COLLECTION & PROCESSING

Levels/Marks	Aspect 1	Aspect 2	Aspect 3
	Recording Raw Data	Processing Raw Data	Presenting Raw Data

DATA

FIELD NAME	VALUE
Expiry date	
Sample Source	
Cell-Type	
Developmental Stage	
Medium	
Serum	
Percent	
Growth	
Temperature	
Doubling-Time	
Selectable Markers	
Propagation	

ANALYSIS

_____
_____
_____
_____
_____
_____

CONCLUSION

_____
_____
_____
_____
_____

ANALYSIS

_____
_____
_____
_____
_____

CONCLUSION

_____
_____
_____
_____
_____
_____
_____
_____

DATA COLLECTION & PROCESSING

Levels/Marks	Aspect 1	Aspect 2	Aspect 3
	Recording Raw Data	Processing Raw Data	Presenting Raw Data

DATA

FIELD NAME	VALUE
Expiry date ·	
Sample Source	
Cell-Type	
Developmental Stage	
Medium	
Serum	
Percent	
Growth	
Temperature	
Doubling-Time	
Selectable Markers	
Propagation	

ANALYSIS

_____
_____
_____
_____
_____

CONCLUSION

_____
_____
_____
_____
_____

ANALYSIS

_____
_____
_____
_____
_____

CONCLUSION

_____
_____
_____
_____
_____
_____
_____

DATA COLLECTION & PROCESSING

Levels/Marks	Aspect 1	Aspect 2	Aspect 3
	Recording Raw Data	Processing Raw Data	Presenting Raw Data

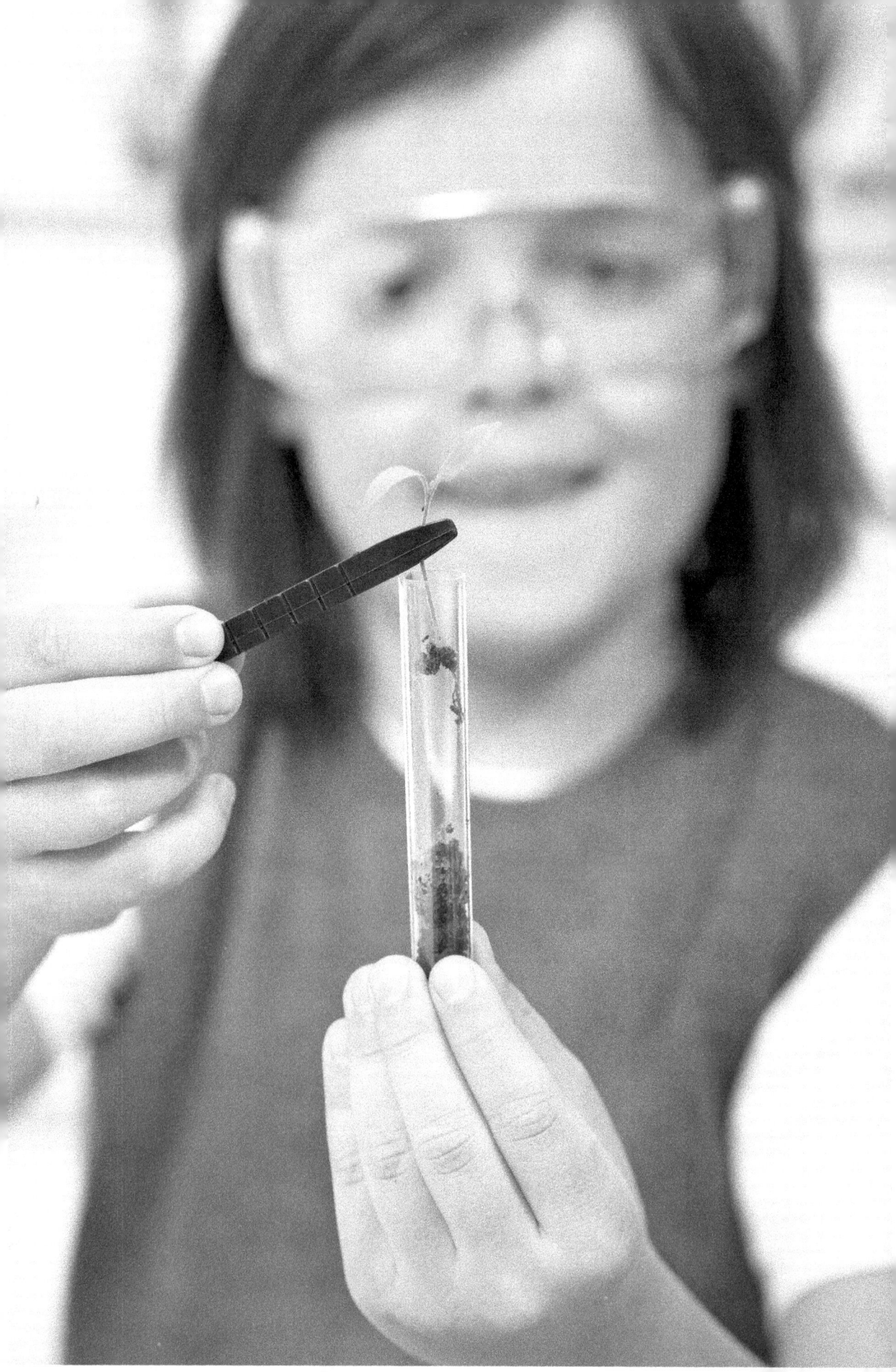

DATA

FIELD NAME	VALUE
Expiry date	
Sample Source	
Cell-Type	
Developmental Stage	
Medium	
Serum	
Percent	
Growth	
Temperature	
Doubling-Time	
Selectable Markers	
Propagation	

ANALYSIS

_____
_____
_____
_____
_____

CONCLUSION

_____
_____
_____
_____
_____

ANALYSIS

_____
_____
_____
_____
_____

CONCLUSION

_____
_____
_____
_____
_____
_____
_____
_____

DATA COLLECTION & PROCESSING

Levels/Marks	Aspect 1	Aspect 2	Aspect 3
	Recording Raw Data	Processing Raw Data	Presenting Raw Data

DATA	
FIELD NAME	VALUE
Expiry date	
Sample Source	
Cell-Type	
Developmental Stage	
Medium	
Serum	
Percent	
Growth	
Temperature	
Doubling-Time	
Selectable Markers	
Propagation	

ANALYSIS

CONCLUSION

ANALYSIS

CONCLUSION

DATA COLLECTION & PROCESSING

Levels/Marks	Aspect 1	Aspect 2	Aspect 3
	Recording Raw Data	Processing Raw Data	Presenting Raw Data

DATA

FIELD NAME	VALUE
Expiry date	
Sample Source	
Cell-Type	
Developmental Stage	
Medium	
Serum	
Percent	
Growth	
Temperature	
Doubling-Time	
Selectable Markers	
Propagation	

ANALYSIS

_____
_____
_____
_____
_____

CONCLUSION

_____
_____
_____
_____
_____

ANALYSIS

_____
_____
_____
_____
_____

CONCLUSION

_____
_____
_____
_____
_____
_____
_____

DATA COLLECTION & PROCESSING

Levels/Marks	Aspect 1	Aspect 2	Aspect 3
	Recording Raw Data	Processing Raw Data	Presenting Raw Data

DATA	
FIELD NAME	VALUE
Expiry date	
Sample Source	
Cell-Type	
Developmental Stage	
Medium	
Serum	
Percent	
Growth	
Temperature	
Doubling-Time	
Selectable Markers	
Propagation	

ANALYSIS

_____
_____
_____
_____
_____

CONCLUSION

_____
_____
_____
_____
_____
_____

ANALYSIS

_____
_____
_____
_____
_____
_____

CONCLUSION

_____
_____
_____
_____
_____
_____
_____
_____
_____

DATA COLLECTION & PROCESSING

Levels/Marks	Aspect 1	Aspect 2	Aspect 3
	Recording Raw Data	Processing Raw Data	Presenting Raw Data

DATA

FIELD NAME	VALUE
Expiry date	
Sample Source	
Cell-Type	
Developmental Stage	
Medium	
Serum	
Percent	
Growth	
Temperature	
Doubling-Time	
Selectable Markers	
Propagation	

ANALYSIS

_____
_____
_____
_____
_____

CONCLUSION

_____
_____
_____
_____
_____

ANALYSIS

_____
_____
_____
_____
_____

CONCLUSION

_____
_____
_____
_____
_____
_____
_____
_____

DATA COLLECTION & PROCESSING

Levels/Marks	Aspect 1	Aspect 2	Aspect 3
	Recording Raw Data	Processing Raw Data	Presenting Raw Data

DATA

FIELD NAME	VALUE
Expiry date	
Sample Source	
Cell-Type	
Developmental Stage	
Medium	
Serum	
Percent	
Growth	
Temperature	
Doubling-Time	
Selectable Markers	
Propagation	

ANALYSIS

_____
_____
_____
_____
_____

CONCLUSION

_____
_____
_____
_____
_____
_____

ANALYSIS

_____
_____
_____
_____
_____
_____

CONCLUSION

_____
_____
_____
_____
_____
_____
_____
_____

DATA COLLECTION & PROCESSING

Levels/Marks	Aspect 1	Aspect 2	Aspect 3
	Recording Raw Data	Processing Raw Data	Presenting Raw Data

DATA

FIELD NAME	VALUE
Expiry date	
Sample Source	
Cell-Type	
Developmental Stage	
Medium	
Serum	
Percent	
Growth	
Temperature	
Doubling-Time	
Selectable Markers	
Propagation	

ANALYSIS

_____
_____
_____
_____
_____

CONCLUSION

_____
_____
_____
_____
_____

ANALYSIS

_____
_____
_____
_____
_____

CONCLUSION

_____
_____
_____
_____
_____
_____
_____
_____

DATA COLLECTION & PROCESSING

Levels/Marks	Aspect 1	Aspect 2	Aspect 3
	Recording Raw Data	Processing Raw Data	Presenting Raw Data

DATA

FIELD NAME	VALUE
Expiry date	
Sample Source	
Cell-Type	
Developmental Stage	
Medium	
Serum	
Percent	
Growth	
Temperature	
Doubling-Time	
Selectable Markers	
Propagation	

ANALYSIS

_____
_____
_____
_____
_____

CONCLUSION

_____
_____
_____
_____
_____

ANALYSIS

_____
_____
_____
_____
_____

CONCLUSION

_____
_____
_____
_____
_____
_____
_____
_____

DATA COLLECTION & PROCESSING

Levels/Marks	Aspect 1	Aspect 2	Aspect 3
	Recording Raw Data	Processing Raw Data	Presenting Raw Data

DATA

FIELD NAME	VALUE
Expiry date	
Sample Source	
Cell-Type	
Developmental Stage	
Medium	
Serum	
Percent	
Growth	
Temperature	
Doubling-Time	
Selectable Markers	
Propagation	

ANALYSIS

_____
_____
_____
_____
_____

CONCLUSION

_____
_____
_____
_____
_____

ANALYSIS

_____
_____
_____
_____
_____

CONCLUSION

_____
_____
_____
_____
_____
_____
_____
_____

DATA COLLECTION & PROCESSING

Levels/Marks	Aspect 1	Aspect 2	Aspect 3
	Recording Raw Data	Processing Raw Data	Presenting Raw Data

DATA

FIELD NAME	VALUE
Expiry date	
Sample Source	
Cell-Type	
Developmental Stage	
Medium	
Serum	
Percent	
Growth	
Temperature	
Doubling-Time	
Selectable Markers	
Propagation	

ANALYSIS

_____
_____
_____
_____
_____

CONCLUSION

_____
_____
_____
_____
_____

ANALYSIS

_____
_____
_____
_____
_____

CONCLUSION

_____
_____
_____
_____
_____
_____
_____

DATA COLLECTION & PROCESSING

Levels/Marks	Aspect 1	Aspect 2	Aspect 3
	Recording Raw Data	Processing Raw Data	Presenting Raw Data

DATA	
FIELD NAME	VALUE
Expiry date	
Sample Source	
Cell-Type	
Developmental Stage	
Medium	
Serum	
Percent	
Growth	
Temperature	
Doubling-Time	
Selectable Markers	
Propagation	

ANALYSIS

_____
_____
_____
_____
_____

CONCLUSION

_____
_____
_____
_____
_____
_____

ANALYSIS

_____
_____
_____
_____
_____

CONCLUSION

_____
_____
_____
_____
_____
_____
_____
_____

DATA COLLECTION & PROCESSING

Levels/Marks	Aspect 1	Aspect 2	Aspect 3
	Recording Raw Data	Processing Raw Data	Presenting Raw Data

DATA	
FIELD NAME	VALUE
Expiry date	
Sample Source	
Cell-Type	
Developmental Stage	
Medium	
Serum	
Percent	
Growth	
Temperature	
Doubling-Time	
Selectable Markers	
Propagation	

ANALYSIS

_____
_____
_____
_____
_____

CONCLUSION

_____
_____
_____
_____
_____

ANALYSIS

_____
_____
_____
_____
_____

CONCLUSION

_____
_____
_____
_____
_____
_____
_____

DATA COLLECTION & PROCESSING

Levels/Marks	Aspect 1	Aspect 2	Aspect 3
	Recording Raw Data	Processing Raw Data	Presenting Raw Data

DATA

FIELD NAME	VALUE
Expiry date	
Sample Source	
Cell-Type	
Developmental Stage	
Medium	
Serum	
Percent	
Growth	
Temperature	
Doubling-Time	
Selectable Markers	
Propagation	

ANALYSIS

_____
_____
_____
_____
_____

CONCLUSION

_____
_____
_____
_____
_____
_____

ANALYSIS

_____
_____
_____
_____
_____
_____

CONCLUSION

_____
_____
_____
_____
_____
_____
_____
_____

DATA COLLECTION & PROCESSING

Levels/Marks	Aspect 1	Aspect 2	Aspect 3
	Recording Raw Data	Processing Raw Data	Presenting Raw Data

DATA

FIELD NAME	VALUE
Expiry date	
Sample Source	
Cell-Type	
Developmental Stage	
Medium	
Serum	
Percent	
Growth	
Temperature	
Doubling-Time	
Selectable Markers	
Propagation	

ANALYSIS

_____
_____
_____
_____
_____

CONCLUSION

_____
_____
_____
_____
_____
_____

ANALYSIS

_____
_____
_____
_____
_____

CONCLUSION

_____
_____
_____
_____
_____
_____
_____
_____

DATA COLLECTION & PROCESSING

Levels/Marks	Aspect 1	Aspect 2	Aspect 3
	Recording Raw Data	Processing Raw Data	Presenting Raw Data

DATA

FIELD NAME	VALUE
Expiry date	
Sample Source	
Cell-Type	
Developmental Stage	
Medium	
Serum	
Percent	
Growth	
Temperature	
Doubling-Time	
Selectable Markers	
Propagation	

ANALYSIS

_____
_____
_____
_____
_____

CONCLUSION

_____
_____
_____
_____
_____

ANALYSIS

_____
_____
_____
_____
_____

CONCLUSION

_____
_____
_____
_____
_____
_____
_____
_____

DATA COLLECTION & PROCESSING

Levels/Marks	Aspect 1	Aspect 2	Aspect 3
	Recording Raw Data	Processing Raw Data	Presenting Raw Data

DATA

FIELD NAME	VALUE
Expiry date	
Sample Source	
Cell-Type	
Developmental Stage	
Medium	
Serum	
Percent	
Growth	
Temperature	
Doubling-Time	
Selectable Markers	
Propagation	

ANALYSIS

_____
_____
_____
_____
_____

CONCLUSION

_____
_____
_____
_____
_____

ANALYSIS

_____
_____
_____
_____
_____

CONCLUSION

_____
_____
_____
_____
_____
_____
_____

DATA COLLECTION & PROCESSING

Levels/Marks	Aspect 1	Aspect 2	Aspect 3
	Recording Raw Data	Processing Raw Data	Presenting Raw Data

DATA

FIELD NAME	VALUE
Expiry date	
Sample Source	
Cell-Type	
Developmental Stage	
Medium	
Serum	
Percent	
Growth	
Temperature	
Doubling-Time	
Selectable Markers	
Propagation	

ANALYSIS

_____
_____
_____
_____
_____

CONCLUSION

_____
_____
_____
_____
_____

ANALYSIS

_____
_____
_____
_____
_____

CONCLUSION

_____
_____
_____
_____
_____
_____
_____
_____

DATA COLLECTION & PROCESSING

Levels/Marks	Aspect 1	Aspect 2	Aspect 3
	Recording Raw Data	Processing Raw Data	Presenting Raw Data

DATA	
FIELD NAME	VALUE
Expiry date	
Sample Source	
Cell-Type	
Developmental Stage	
Medium	
Serum	
Percent	
Growth	
Temperature	
Doubling-Time	
Selectable Markers	
Propagation	

ANALYSIS

_____
_____
_____
_____
_____

CONCLUSION

_____
_____
_____
_____
_____
_____

ANALYSIS

_____
_____
_____
_____
_____
_____

CONCLUSION

_____
_____
_____
_____
_____
_____
_____
_____
_____

DATA COLLECTION & PROCESSING

Levels/Marks	Aspect 1	Aspect 2	Aspect 3
	Recording Raw Data	Processing Raw Data	Presenting Raw Data

DATA

FIELD NAME	VALUE
Expiry date	
Sample Source	
Cell-Type	
Developmental Stage	
Medium	
Serum	
Percent	
Growth	
Temperature	
Doubling-Time	
Selectable Markers	
Propagation	

ANALYSIS

_____
_____
_____
_____
_____

CONCLUSION

_____
_____
_____
_____
_____

ANALYSIS

_____
_____
_____
_____
_____

CONCLUSION

_____
_____
_____
_____
_____
_____

DATA COLLECTION & PROCESSING

Levels/Marks	Aspect 1	Aspect 2	Aspect 3
	Recording Raw Data	Processing Raw Data	Presenting Raw Data

DATA

FIELD NAME	VALUE
Expiry date	
Sample Source	
Cell-Type	
Developmental Stage	
Medium	
Serum	
Percent	
Growth	
Temperature	
Doubling-Time	
Selectable Markers	
Propagation	

ANALYSIS

_____
_____
_____
_____
_____

CONCLUSION

_____
_____
_____
_____
_____
_____

ANALYSIS

_____
_____
_____
_____
_____
_____

CONCLUSION

_____
_____
_____
_____
_____
_____
_____
_____
_____

DATA COLLECTION & PROCESSING

Levels/Marks	Aspect 1	Aspect 2	Aspect 3
	Recording Raw Data	Processing Raw Data	Presenting Raw Data

DATA

FIELD NAME	VALUE
Expiry date	
Sample Source	
Cell-Type	
Developmental Stage	
Medium	
Serum	
Percent	
Growth	
Temperature	
Doubling-Time	
Selectable Markers	
Propagation	

ANALYSIS

_____
_____
_____
_____
_____

CONCLUSION

_____
_____
_____
_____
_____

ANALYSIS

_____
_____
_____
_____
_____

CONCLUSION

_____
_____
_____
_____
_____
_____
_____
_____

DATA COLLECTION & PROCESSING

Levels/Marks	Aspect 1	Aspect 2	Aspect 3
	Recording Raw Data	Processing Raw Data	Presenting Raw Data

DATA

FIELD NAME	VALUE
Expiry date	
Sample Source	
Cell-Type	
Developmental Stage	
Medium	
Serum	
Percent	
Growth	
Temperature	
Doubling-Time	
Selectable Markers	
Propagation	

ANALYSIS

_____
_____
_____
_____
_____

CONCLUSION

_____
_____
_____
_____
_____

ANALYSIS

_____
_____
_____
_____
_____

CONCLUSION

_____
_____
_____
_____
_____
_____
_____
_____

DATA COLLECTION & PROCESSING

Levels/Marks	Aspect 1	Aspect 2	Aspect 3
	Recording Raw Data	Processing Raw Data	Presenting Raw Data

DATA

FIELD NAME	VALUE
Expiry date	
Sample Source	
Cell-Type	
Developmental Stage	
Medium	
Serum	
Percent	
Growth	
Temperature	
Doubling-Time	
Selectable Markers	
Propagation	

ANALYSIS

CONCLUSION

ANALYSIS

CONCLUSION

DATA COLLECTION & PROCESSING

Levels/Marks	Aspect 1	Aspect 2	Aspect 3
	Recording Raw Data	Processing Raw Data	Presenting Raw Data

DATA

FIELD NAME	VALUE
Expiry date	
Sample Source	
Cell-Type	
Developmental Stage	
Medium	
Serum	
Percent	
Growth	
Temperature	
Doubling-Time	
Selectable Markers	
Propagation	

ANALYSIS

_____
_____
_____
_____
_____

CONCLUSION

_____
_____
_____
_____
_____

ANALYSIS

_____
_____
_____
_____
_____

CONCLUSION

_____
_____
_____
_____
_____
_____
_____
_____

DATA COLLECTION & PROCESSING

Levels/Marks	Aspect 1	Aspect 2	Aspect 3
	Recording Raw Data	Processing Raw Data	Presenting Raw Data

DATA

FIELD NAME	VALUE
Expiry date	
Sample Source	
Cell-Type	
Developmental Stage	
Medium	
Serum	
Percent	
Growth	
Temperature	
Doubling-Time	
Selectable Markers	
Propagation	

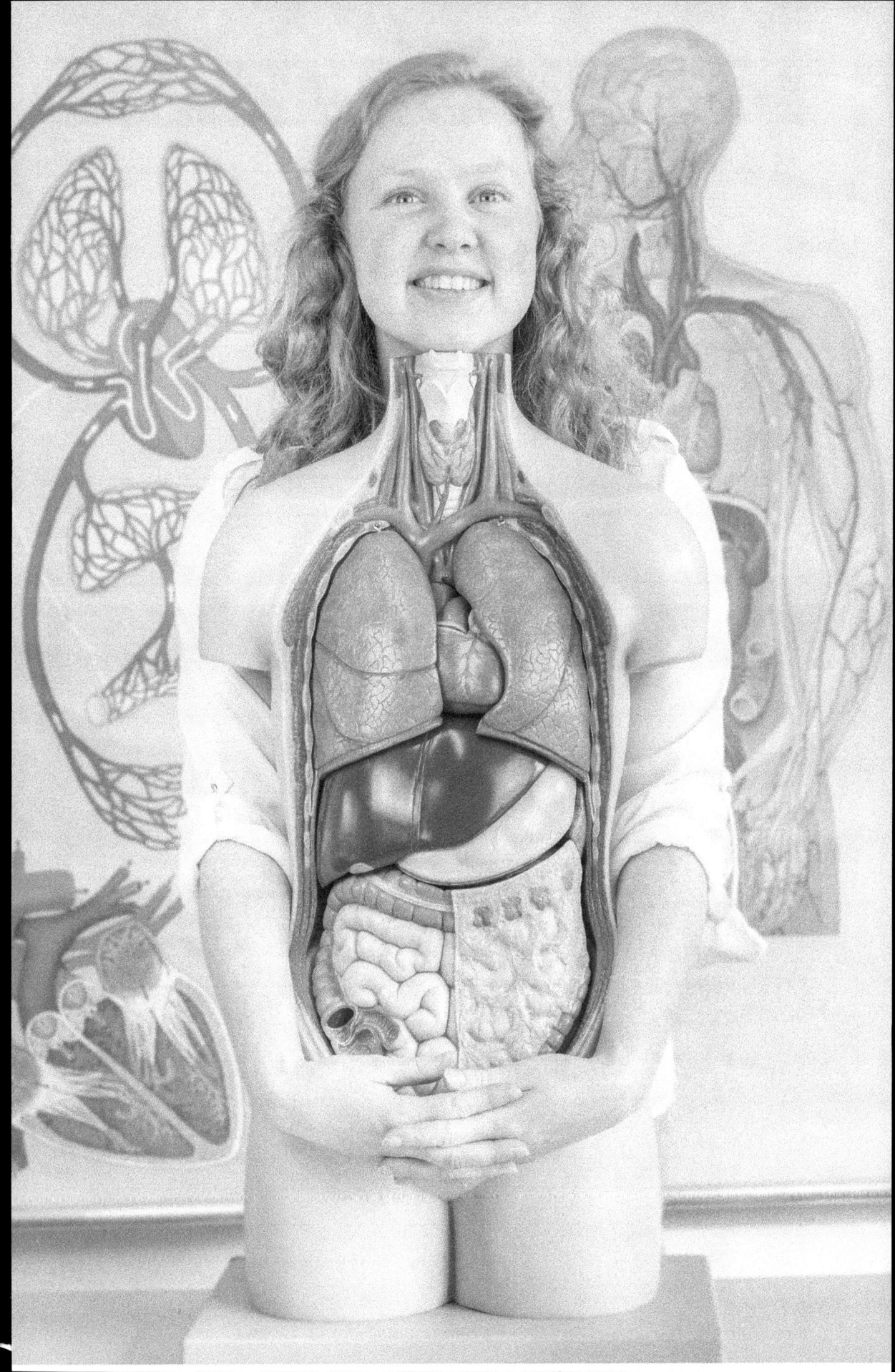

ANALYSIS

_____
_____
_____
_____
_____

CONCLUSION

_____
_____
_____
_____
_____

ANALYSIS

_____
_____
_____
_____
_____

CONCLUSION

_____
_____
_____
_____
_____
_____
_____
_____

DATA COLLECTION & PROCESSING

Levels/Marks	Aspect 1	Aspect 2	Aspect 3
	Recording Raw Data	Processing Raw Data	Presenting Raw Data

you are :
BRAVER than
you believe
Stonger than
you seem
Faster than
you Think.

Run ∘ Stretch ∘ Breath
Sweat ∘ Drink ∘ Relax ∘ Live

Time

_____ Date

Distance

Pace

Route

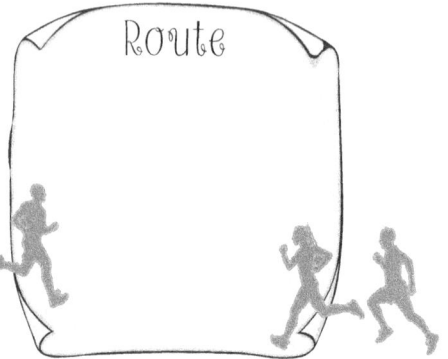

Running Buddies :

Notes :

You are :
BRAVER than
you believe
STONGER than
you seem
FASTER than
you Think.

Run ∘ Stretch ∘ Breath ∘ Sweat ∘ Drink ∘ Relax ∘ Live

You are :
Braver than
you believe
Stonger than
you seem
Faster than
you Think.

Run ◦ Stretch ◦ Breath
Sweat ◦ Drink ◦ Relax ◦ Live

Time

_____ Date

Distance

Pace

Route

Running Buddies :

Notes :

You are :
BRAVER than
you believe
STONGER than
you seem
FASTER than
you Think.

Run ○ Stretch ○ Breath ○ Sweat ○ Drink ○ Relax ○ Live

you are :
BRAVER than
   you believe
Stonger than
   you seem
Faster than
   you Think.

Run ∘ Stretch ∘ Breath
Sweat ∘ Drink ∘ Relax ∘ Live

Time

_____ Date

Distance

Pace

Route

Running Buddies :

Notes :

You are :
BRAVER than
     you believe
STONGER than
      you seem
FASTER than
     you Think.

Run ○ Stretch ○ Breath ○ Sweat ○ Drink ○ Relax ○ Live

You are :
BRAVER than you believe
Stonger than you seem
Faster than you Think.

Run ◦ Stretch ◦ Breath
Sweat ◦ Drink ◦ Relax ◦ Live

Time

_____ Date

Distance

Pace

Route

Running Buddies :

Notes :

You are :
BRAVER than
you believe
Stonger than
you seem
Faster than
you Think.

Run ∘ Stretch ∘ Breath ∘ Sweat ∘ Drink ∘ Relax ∘ Live

YOU ARE :

BRAVER than
    you believe

STONGER than
    you seem

FASTER than
    you Think.

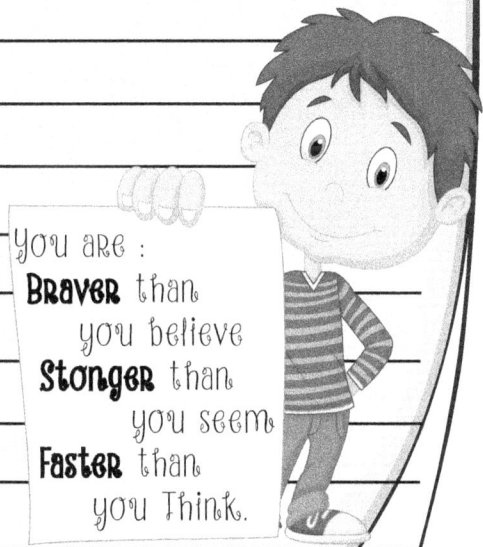

Run ○ Stretch ○ Breath
Sweat ○ Drink ○ Relax ○ Live

Time

_____ Date

Distance

Pace

Route

Running Buddies :

Notes :

You are :
BRAVER than
    you believe
Stonger than
    you seem
Faster than
    you Think.

Run ∘ Stretch ∘ Breath ∘ Sweat ∘ Drink ∘ Relax ∘ Live

You are :
BRAVER than
          you believe
Stonger than
          you seem
Faster than
          you Think.

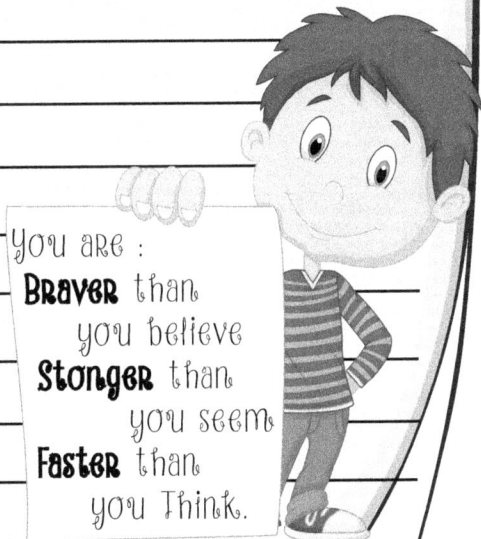

Run ∘ Stretch ∘ Breath
Sweat ∘ Drink ∘ Relax ∘ Live

Time

_____ Date

Distance

Pace

Route

Running Buddies :

Notes :

You are :
BRAVER than
  you believe
Stonger than
  you seem
Faster than
  you Think.

Run ∘ Stretch ∘ Breath ∘ Sweat ∘ Drink ∘ Relax ∘ Live

you are :
Braver than
you believe
Stonger than
you seem
Faster than
you Think.

Run ∘ Stretch ∘ Breath
Sweat ∘ Drink ∘ Relax ∘ Live

Time

_____ Date

Distance

Pace

Route

Running Buddies :

Notes :

You are :
BRAVER than
you believe
STONGER than
you seem
Faster than
you Think.

Run ○ Stretch ○ Breath ○ Sweat ○ Drink ○ Relax ○ Live

you are :
BRAVER than
you believe
Stonger than
you seem
Faster than
you Think.

Run ◦ Stretch ◦ Breath
Sweat ◦ Drink ◦ Relax ◦ Live

Time

_____ Date

Distance

Pace

Route

Running Buddies :

Notes :

You are :
Braver than
you believe
Stonger than
you seem
Faster than
you Think.

Run ○ Stretch ○ Breath ○ Sweat ○ Drink ○ Relax ○ Live

You are :
BRAVER than
you believe
STONGER than
you seem
FASTER than
you Think.

Run ∘ Stretch ∘ Breath
Sweat ∘ Drink ∘ Relax ∘ Live

Time

_____ Date

Distance

Pace

Route

Running Buddies :

Notes :

You are :
BRAVER than
you believe
STONGER than
you seem
Faster than
you Think.

Run ○ Stretch ○ Breath ○ Sweat ○ Drink ○ Relax ○ Live

You are :
Braver than
you believe
Stonger than
you seem
Faster than
you Think.

Run ○ Stretch ○ Breath
Sweat ○ Drink ○ Relax ○ Live

Time

_____ Date

Distance

Pace

Route

Running Buddies :

Notes :

You are :
BRAVER than
      you believe
Stonger than
      you seem
Faster than
      you Think.

Run ◦ Stretch ◦ Breath ◦ Sweat ◦ Drink ◦ Relax ◦ Live

You are :
BRAVER than
         you believe
Stonger than
         you seem
Faster than
         you Think.

Run ◦ Stretch ◦ Breath
Sweat ◦ Drink ◦ Relax ◦ Live

Time

_____ Date

Distance

Pace

Route

Running Buddies :

Notes :

You are :
BRAVER than
         you believe
STONGER than
         you seem
FASTER than
         you Think.

Run ∘ Stretch ∘ Breath ∘ Sweat ∘ Drink ∘ Relax ∘ Live

YOU ARE :
BRAVER than
you believe
STONGER than
you seem
FASTER than
you Think.

Run ○ Stretch ○ Breath
Sweat ○ Drink ○ Relax ○ Live

Time

_____ Date

Distance

Pace

Route

Running Buddies :

Notes :

You are :
BRAVER than
you believe
Stonger than
you seem
Faster than
you Think.

Run ◦ Stretch ◦ Breath ◦ Sweat ◦ Drink ◦ Relax ◦ Live

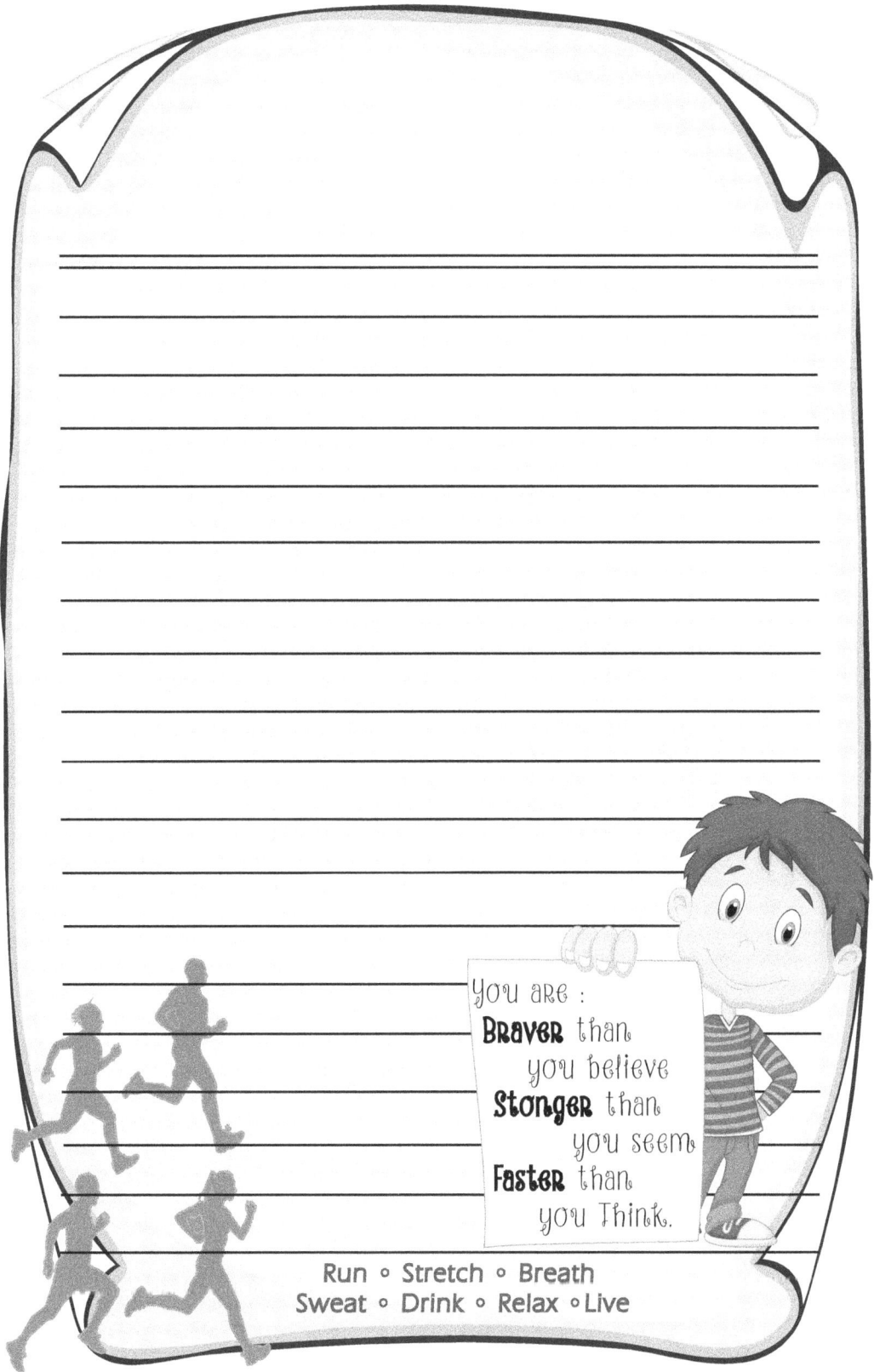

You are :
BRAVER than
          you believe
Stonger than
          you seem
Faster than
          you Think.

Run ○ Stretch ○ Breath
Sweat ○ Drink ○ Relax ○ Live

Time

_____ Date

Distance

Pace

Route

Running Buddies :

Notes :

You are :
BRAVER than
you believe
STONGER than
you seem
FASTER than
you Think.

Run ○ Stretch ○ Breath ○ Sweat ○ Drink ○ Relax ○ Live

YOU ARE :
BRAVER than
you believe
STONGER than
you seem
FASTER than
you Think.

Run ○ Stretch ○ Breath
Sweat ○ Drink ○ Relax ○ Live

Time

_____ Date

Distance

Pace

Route

Running Buddies :

Notes :

You are :
BRAVER than
    you believe
Stonger than
    you seem
Faster than
    you Think.

Run ∘ Stretch ∘ Breath ∘ Sweat ∘ Drink ∘ Relax ∘ Live

You are :

BRAVER than
        you believe
Stonger than
        you seem
Faster than
        you Think.

Run ○ Stretch ○ Breath
Sweat ○ Drink ○ Relax ○ Live

Time

_____ Date

Distance

Pace

Route

Running Buddies :

Notes :

You are :
Braver than
you believe
Stonger than
you seem
Faster than
you Think.

Run ◦ Stretch ◦ Breath ◦ Sweat ◦ Drink ◦ Relax ◦ Live

you are :
BRAVER than
    you believe
Stonger than
    you seem
Faster than
    you Think.

Run ○ Stretch ○ Breath
Sweat ○ Drink ○ Relax ○ Live

Time

_____ Date

Distance

Pace

Route

Running Buddies :

Notes :

YOU ARE :
BRAVER than
    you believe
STONGER than
    you seem
FASTER than
    you Think.

Run ◦ Stretch ◦ Breath ◦ Sweat ◦ Drink ◦ Relax ◦ Live

YOU ARE :
BRAVER than
you believe
Stonger than
you seem
Faster than
you Think.

Run ∘ Stretch ∘ Breath
Sweat ∘ Drink ∘ Relax ∘ Live

Time

_____ Date

Distance

Pace

Route

Running Buddies :

Notes :

You are :
BRAVER than
    you believe
STONGER than
    you seem
FASTER than
    you Think.

Run ◦ Stretch ◦ Breath ◦ Sweat ◦ Drink ◦ Relax ◦ Live

You are :
Braver than
you believe
Stonger than
you seem
Faster than
you Think.

Run ○ Stretch ○ Breath
Sweat ○ Drink ○ Relax ○ Live

Time

_____ Date

Distance

Pace

Route

Running Buddies :

Notes :

You are :
BRAVER than
you believe
STONGER than
you seem
FASTER than
you Think.

Run ∘ Stretch ∘ Breath ∘ Sweat ∘ Drink ∘ Relax ∘ Live

you are :
BRAVER than
    you believe
Stonger than
    you seem
Faster than
    you Think.

Run ○ Stretch ○ Breath
Sweat ○ Drink ○ Relax ○ Live

Time

_____ Date

Distance

Pace

Route

Running Buddies :

Notes :

you are :
BRAVER than
    you believe
STONGER than
    you seem
FASTER than
    you Think.

Run ◦ Stretch ◦ Breath ◦ Sweat ◦ Drink ◦ Relax ◦ Live

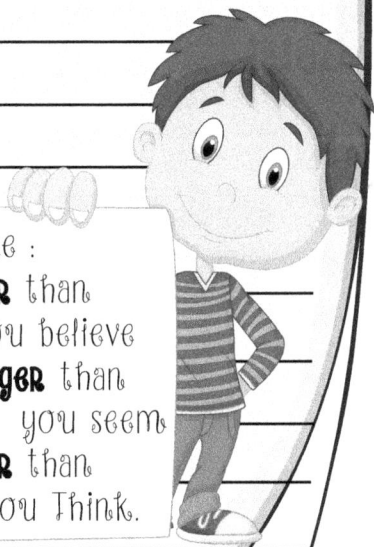

You are :
BRAVER than
    you believe
Stonger than
    you seem
Faster than
    you Think.

Run ○ Stretch ○ Breath
Sweat ○ Drink ○ Relax ○ Live

Time

_____ Date

Distance

Pace

Route

Running Buddies :

Notes :

You are :
BRAVER than
you believe
STONGER than
you seem
FASTER than
you Think.

Run ◦ Stretch ◦ Breath ◦ Sweat ◦ Drink ◦ Relax ◦ Live

You are :
BRAVER than
you believe
Stonger than
you seem
Faster than
you Think.

Run ○ Stretch ○ Breath
Sweat ○ Drink ○ Relax ○ Live

Time

_____ Date

Distance

Pace

Route

Running Buddies :

Notes :

You are :
BRAVER than
      you believe
STONGER than
      you seem
FASTER than
      you Think.

Run ∘ Stretch ∘ Breath ∘ Sweat ∘ Drink ∘ Relax ∘ Live

You are :
Braver than
  you believe
Stonger than
  you seem
Faster than
  you Think.

Run ◦ Stretch ◦ Breath
Sweat ◦ Drink ◦ Relax ◦ Live

Time

_____ Date

Distance

Pace

Route

Running Buddies :

Notes :

You are :
BRAVER than
you believe
STONGER than
you seem
FASTER than
you Think.

Run ∘ Stretch ∘ Breath ∘ Sweat ∘ Drink ∘ Relax ∘ Live

You are :
BRAVER than
you believe
Stonger than
you seem
Faster than
you Think.

Run ◦ Stretch ◦ Breath
Sweat ◦ Drink ◦ Relax ◦ Live

Time

_____ Date

Distance

Pace

Route

Running Buddies :

Notes :

you are :
BRAVER than
you believe
Stonger than
you seem
Faster than
you Think.

Run ○ Stretch ○ Breath ○ Sweat ○ Drink ○ Relax ○ Live

You are :
BRAVER than
you believe
Stonger than
you seem
Faster than
you Think.

Run ∘ Stretch ∘ Breath
Sweat ∘ Drink ∘ Relax ∘ Live

Time

_____ Date

Distance

Pace

Route

Running Buddies :

Notes :

You are :
BRAVER than
you believe
STONGER than
you seem
FASTER than
you Think.

Run ◦ Stretch ◦ Breath ◦ Sweat ◦ Drink ◦ Relax ◦ Live

_____
_____
_____
_____
_____
_____
_____
_____
_____
_____
_____
_____
_____
_____
_____
_____

YOU ARE :
BRAVER than
            you believe
Stonger than
            you seem
Faster than
            you Think.

Run ◦ Stretch ◦ Breath
Sweat ◦ Drink ◦ Relax ◦ Live

Time

_____ Date

Distance

Pace

Route

Running Buddies :

Notes :

you are :
BRAVER than
        you believe
STONGER than
        you seem
Faster than
        you Think.

Run ○ Stretch ○ Breath ○ Sweat ○ Drink ○ Relax ○ Live

you are :

BRAVER than
you believe

Stonger than
you seem

Faster than
you Think.

Run ○ Stretch ○ Breath
Sweat ○ Drink ○ Relax ○ Live

Time

_____ Date

Distance

Pace

Route

Running Buddies :

Notes :

You are :
Braver than
you believe
Stonger than
you seem
Faster than
you Think.

Run ∘ Stretch ∘ Breath ∘ Sweat ∘ Drink ∘ Relax ∘ Live

you are :
BRAVER than
        you believe
Stonger than
        you seem
Faster than
        you Think.

Run ○ Stretch ○ Breath
Sweat ○ Drink ○ Relax ○ Live

Time

_____ Date

Distance

Pace

Route

Running Buddies :

Notes :

You are :
BRAVER than
you believe
STONGER than
you seem
FASTER than
you Think.

Run ○ Stretch ○ Breath ○ Sweat ○ Drink ○ Relax ○ Live

You are :
BRAVER than
you believe
Stonger than
you seem
Faster than
you Think.

Run ∘ Stretch ∘ Breath
Sweat ∘ Drink ∘ Relax ∘ Live

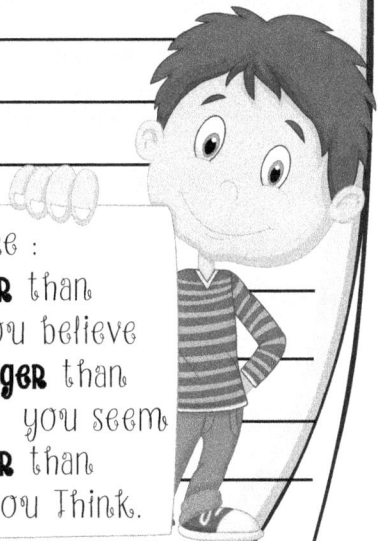

Time

_____ Date

Distance

Pace

Route

Running Buddies :

Notes :

You are :
BRAVER than
        you believe
STONGER than
        you seem
FASTER than
        you Think.

Run ○ Stretch ○ Breath ○ Sweat ○ Drink ○ Relax ○ Live

You are :
BRAVER than
            you believe
STONGER than
            you seem
Faster than
            you Think.

Run ○ Stretch ○ Breath
Sweat ○ Drink ○ Relax ○ Live

Time

_____ Date

Distance

Pace

Route

Running Buddies :

Notes :

You are :
BRAVER than
    you believe
STONGER than
    you seem
FASTER than
    you Think.

Run ∘ Stretch ∘ Breath ∘ Sweat ∘ Drink ∘ Relax ∘ Live

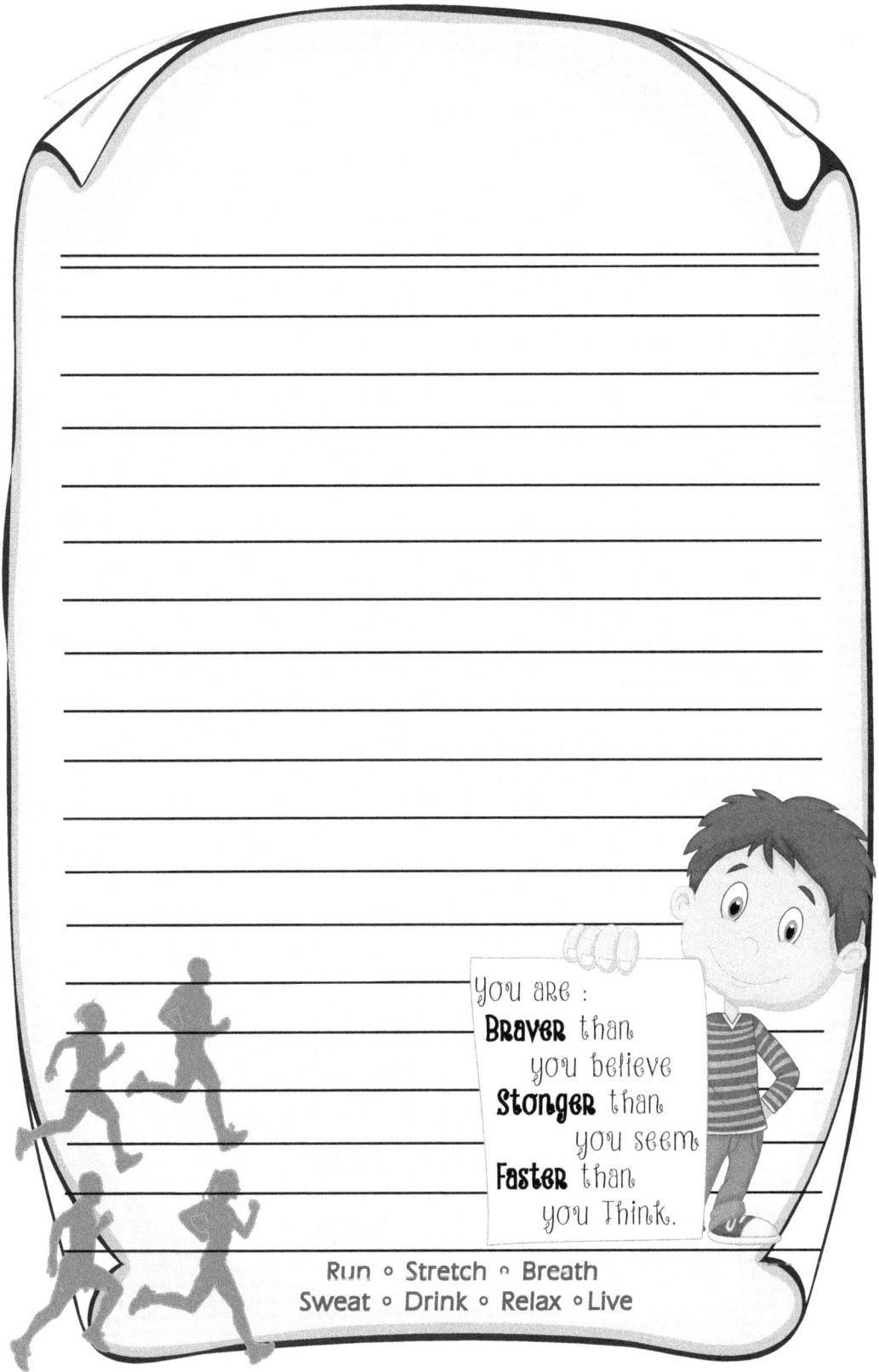

YOU ARE :
BRAVER than
you believe
STONGER than
you seem
Faster than
you Think.

Run ◦ Stretch ◦ Breath
Sweat ◦ Drink ◦ Relax ◦ Live

Time

_____ Date

Distance

Pace

Route

Running Buddies :

Notes :

You are :
BRAVER than
you believe
STONGER than
you seem
FASTER than
you Think.

Run ∘ Stretch ∘ Breath ∘ Sweat ∘ Drink ∘ Relax ∘ Live

You are :

BRAVER than
you believe
STONGER than
you seem
Faster than
you Think.

Run ○ Stretch ○ Breath
Sweat ○ Drink ○ Relax ○ Live

Time

_____ Date

Distance

Pace

Route

Running Buddies :

Notes :

You are :
BRAVER than
you believe
STONGER than
you seem
FASTER than
you Think.

Run ∘ Stretch ∘ Breath ∘ Sweat ∘ Drink ∘ Relax ∘ Live

You are :
BRAVER than
you believe
Stonger than
you seem
Faster than
you Think.

Run ∘ Stretch ∘ Breath
Sweat ∘ Drink ∘ Relax ∘ Live

Time

_____ Date

Distance

Pace

Route

Running Buddies :

Notes :

You are :
BRAVER than
    you believe
STONGER than
    you seem
FASTER than
    you Think.

Run ∘ Stretch ∘ Breath ∘ Sweat ∘ Drink ∘ Relax ∘ Live

You are :
BRAVER than
you believe
STONGER than
you seem
FASTER than
you Think.

Run ∘ Stretch ∘ Breath
Sweat ∘ Drink ∘ Relax ∘ Live

Time

_____ Date

Distance

Pace

Route

Running Buddies :

Notes :

You are :
Braver than
you believe
Stonger than
you seem
Faster than
you Think.

Run ∘ Stretch ∘ Breath ∘ Sweat ∘ Drink ∘ Relax ∘ Live

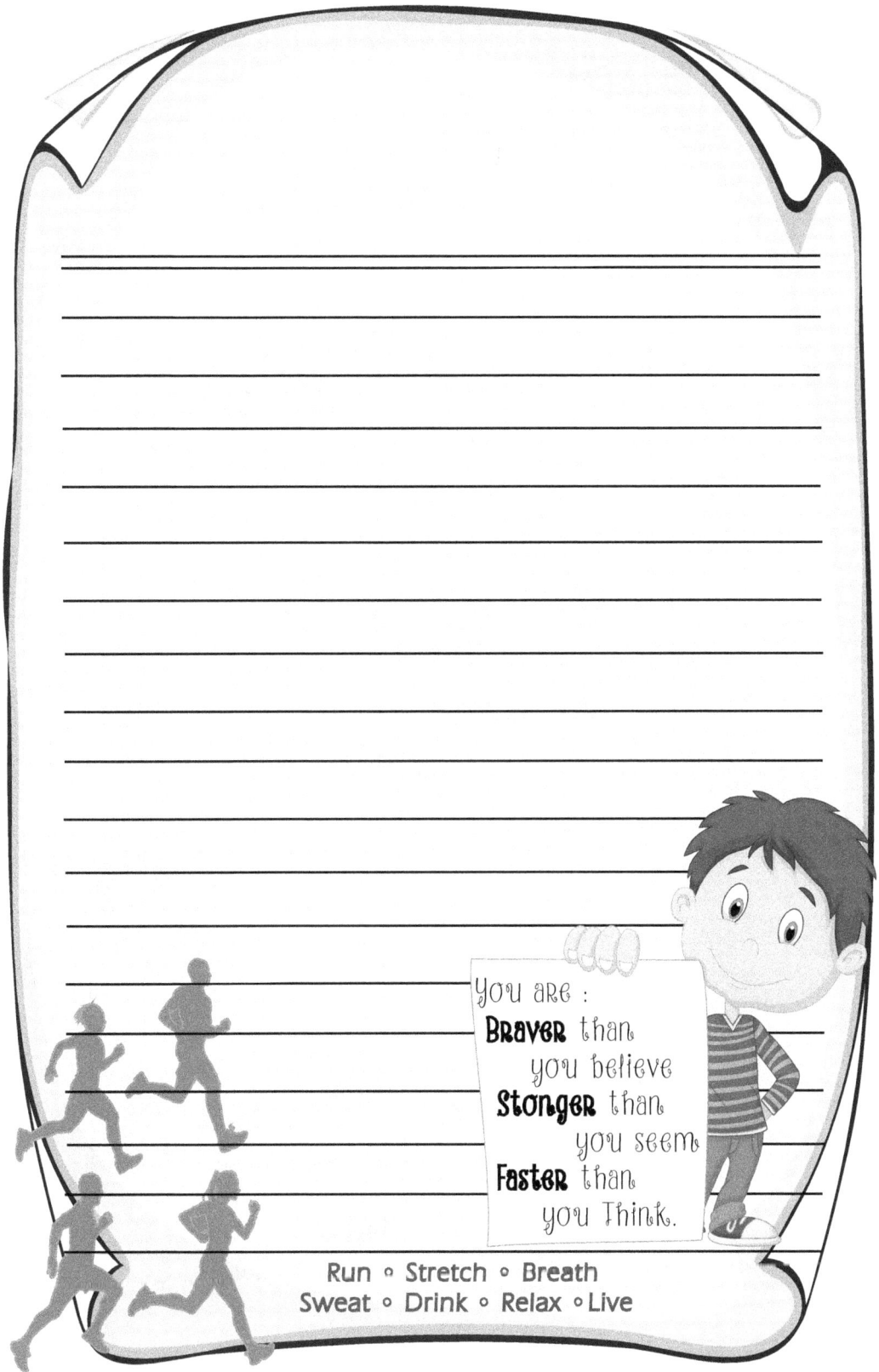

you are :
BRAVER than
you believe
Stonger than
you seem
Faster than
you Think.

Run ∘ Stretch ∘ Breath
Sweat ∘ Drink ∘ Relax ∘ Live

Time

_____ Date

Distance

Pace

Route

Running Buddies :

Notes :

You are :
BRAVER than
  you believe
STONGER than
  you seem
FASTER than
  you Think.

Run ∘ Stretch ∘ Breath ∘ Sweat ∘ Drink ∘ Relax ∘ Live

YOU ARE :

BRAVER than
you believe

STONGER than
you seem

FASTER than
you Think.

Run ∘ Stretch ∘ Breath
Sweat ∘ Drink ∘ Relax ∘ Live

Time

_____ Date

Distance

Pace

Route

Running Buddies :

Notes :

You are :
BRAVER than
     you believe
STONGER than
     you seem
FASTER than
     you Think.

Run ◦ Stretch ◦ Breath ◦ Sweat ◦ Drink ◦ Relax ◦ Live

You are :
BRAVER than
   you believe
Stonger than
   you seem
Faster than
   you Think.

Run ◦ Stretch ◦ Breath
Sweat ◦ Drink ◦ Relax ◦ Live

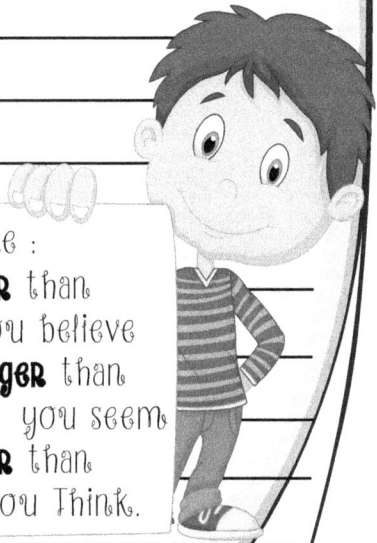

Time

_____ Date

Distance

Pace

Route

Running Buddies :

Notes :

You are :
BRAVER than
     you believe
STONGER than
     you seem
FASTER than
     you Think.

Run ◦ Stretch ◦ Breath ◦ Sweat ◦ Drink ◦ Relax ◦ Live

you are :
BRAVER than
you believe
Stonger than
you seem
Faster than
you Think.

Run ∘ Stretch ∘ Breath
Sweat ∘ Drink ∘ Relax ∘ Live

_____ Date

Time

Distance

Pace

Route

Running Buddies :

Notes :

You are :
BRAVER than
you believe
STONGER than
you seem
FASTER than
you Think.

Run ∘ Stretch ∘ Breath ∘ Sweat ∘ Drink ∘ Relax ∘ Live

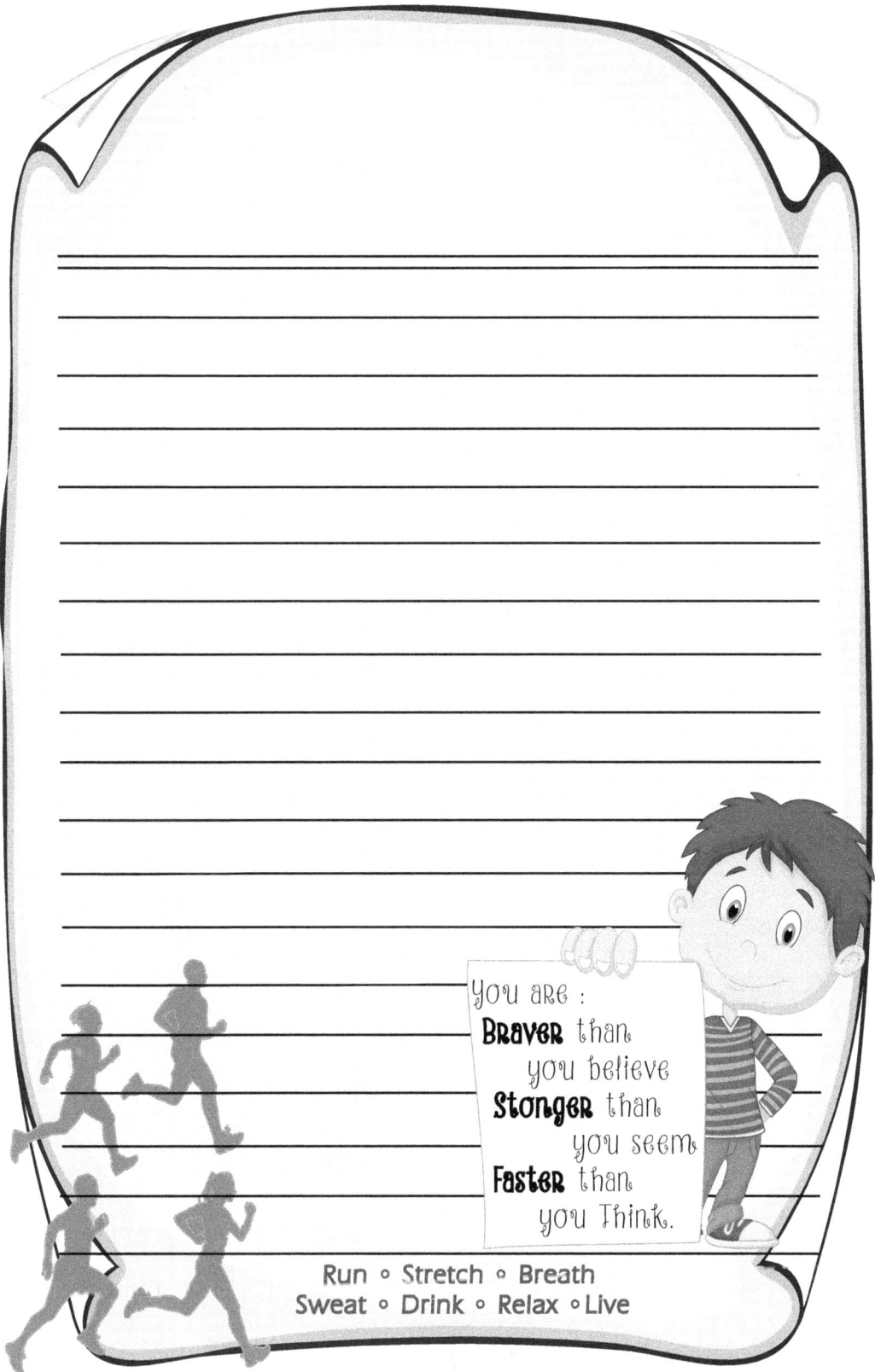

YOU ARE :
BRAVER than
    you believe
STONGER than
    you seem
FASTER than
    you Think.

Run ∘ Stretch ∘ Breath
Sweat ∘ Drink ∘ Relax ∘ Live

Time

_____ Date

Distance

Pace

Route

Running Buddies :

Notes :

You are :
BRAVER than
you believe
STONGER than
you seem
FASTER than
you Think.

Run ○ Stretch ○ Breath ○ Sweat ○ Drink ○ Relax ○ Live

You are :
Braver than
you believe
Stonger than
you seem
Faster than
you Think.

Run ◦ Stretch ◦ Breath
Sweat ◦ Drink ◦ Relax ◦ Live

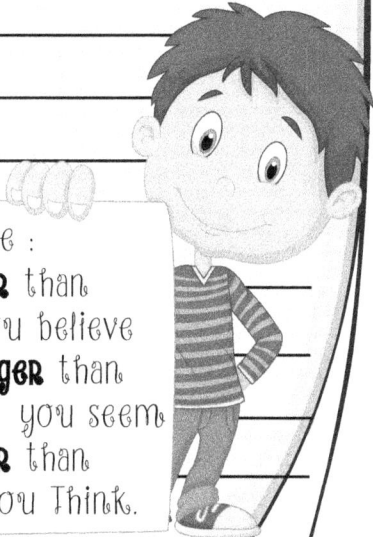

Time

_____ Date

Distance

Pace

Route

Running Buddies :

Notes :

You are :
BRAVER than
    you believe
STONGER than
    you seem
FASTER than
    you Think.

Run ◦ Stretch ◦ Breath ◦ Sweat ◦ Drink ◦ Relax ◦ Live

you are :
BRAVER than
you believe
STONGER than
you seem
FASTER than
you Think.

Run ∘ Stretch ∘ Breath
Sweat ∘ Drink ∘ Relax ∘ Live

Time

_____ Date

Distance

Pace

Route

Running Buddies :

Notes :

You are :
BRAVER than
you believe
STONGER than
you seem
FASTER than
you Think.

Run ○ Stretch ○ Breath ○ Sweat ○ Drink ○ Relax ○ Live

YOU ARE :

BRAVER than
you believe

STONGER than
you seem

Faster than
you Think.

Run ◦ Stretch ◦ Breath
Sweat ◦ Drink ◦ Relax ◦ Live

Time

_____ Date

Distance

Pace

Route

Running Buddies :

Notes :

You are :
BRAVER than you believe
STONGER than you seem
FASTER than you Think.

Run ○ Stretch ○ Breath ○ Sweat ○ Drink ○ Relax ○ Live

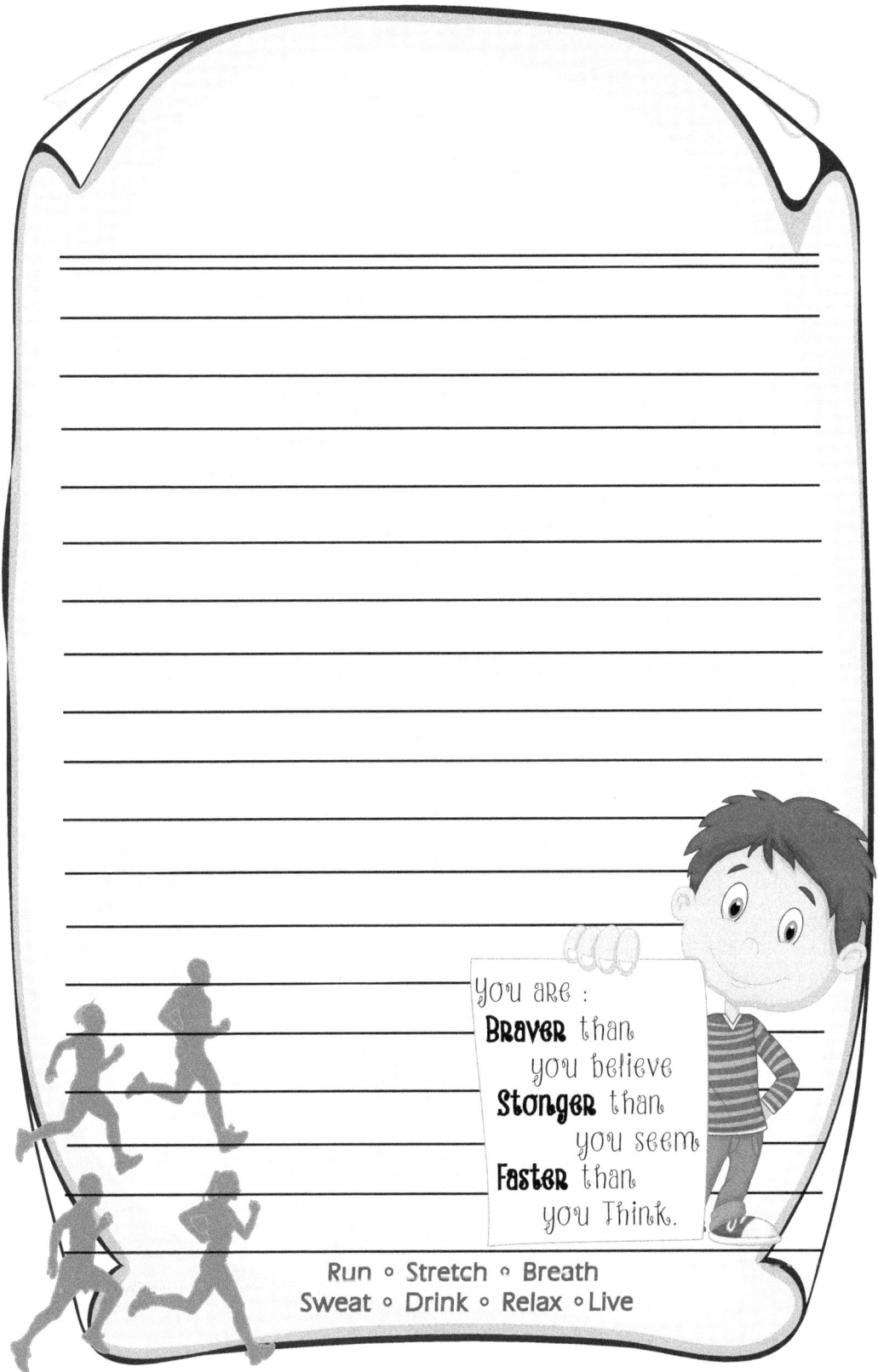

You are :
BRAVER than
you believe
STONGER than
you seem
Faster than
you Think.

Run ∘ Stretch ∘ Breath
Sweat ∘ Drink ∘ Relax ∘ Live

Time

_____ Date

Distance

Pace

Route

Running Buddies :

Notes :

You are :
BRAVER than
you believe
STONGER than
you seem
FASTER than
you Think.

Run ○ Stretch ○ Breath ○ Sweat ○ Drink ○ Relax ○ Live

You are :
Braver than
you believe
Stonger than
you seem
Faster than
you Think.

Run ○ Stretch ○ Breath
Sweat ○ Drink ○ Relax ○ Live

Time

_____ Date

Distance

Pace

Route

Running Buddies :

Notes :

You are :
BRAVER than
you believe
STONGER than
you seem
Faster than
you Think.

Run ○ Stretch ○ Breath ○ Sweat ○ Drink ○ Relax ○ Live

You are :
BRAVER than
      you believe
Stonger than
      you seem
Faster than
      you Think.

Run ∘ Stretch ∘ Breath
Sweat ∘ Drink ∘ Relax ∘ Live

Time

_____ Date

Distance

Pace

Route

Running Buddies :

Notes :

You are :
BRAVER than
you believe
STONGER than
you seem
FASTER than
you Think.

Run ∘ Stretch ∘ Breath ∘ Sweat ∘ Drink ∘ Relax ∘ Live

You are :
BRAVER than
you believe
STONGER than
you seem
FASTER than
you Think.

Run ○ Stretch ○ Breath
Sweat ○ Drink ○ Relax ○ Live

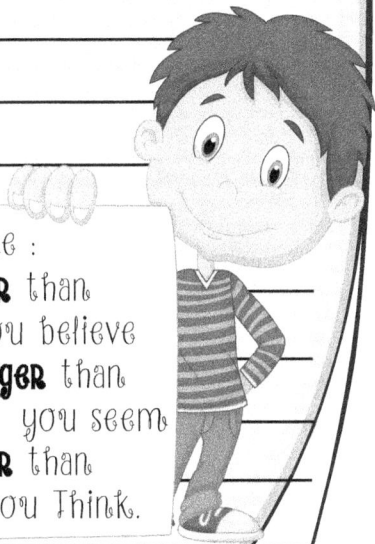

Time

_____ Date

Distance

Pace

Route

Running Buddies :

Notes :

You are :
BRAVER than
you believe
STONGER than
you seem
FASTER than
you Think.

Run ◦ Stretch ◦ Breath ◦ Sweat ◦ Drink ◦ Relax ◦ Live

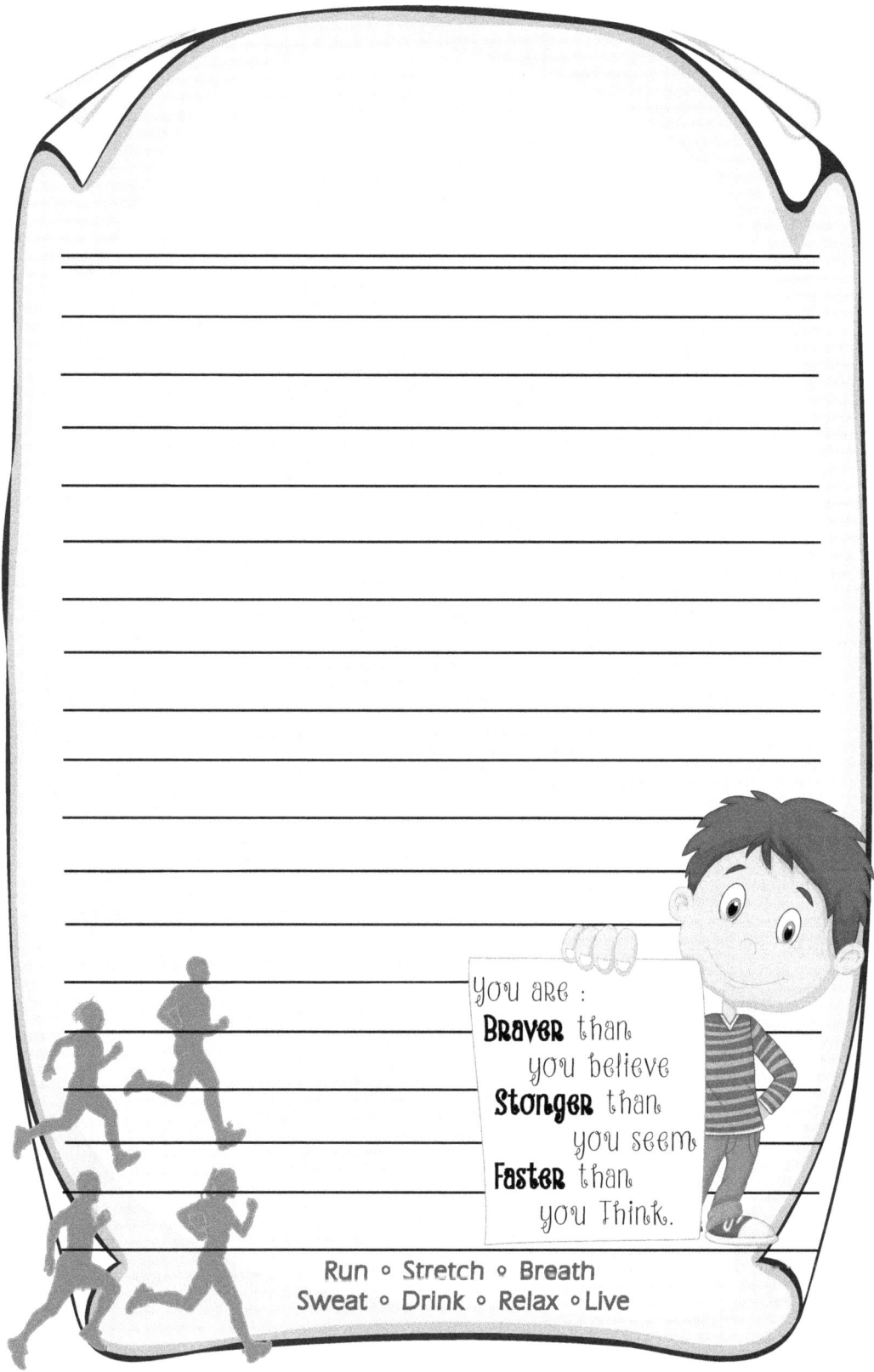

YOU ARE :
BRAVER than
you believe
STONGER than
you seem
FASTER than
you Think.

Run ○ Stretch ○ Breath
Sweat ○ Drink ○ Relax ○ Live

Time

_____ Date

Distance

Pace

Route

Running Buddies :

Notes :

You are :
BRAVER than you believe
STONGER than you seem
FASTER than you Think.

Run ∘ Stretch ∘ Breath ∘ Sweat ∘ Drink ∘ Relax ∘ Live

YOU ARE :
BRAVER than
       you believe
STOnGER than
       you seem
Faster than
       you Think.

Run ◦ Stretch ◦ Breath
Sweat ◦ Drink ◦ Relax ◦ Live

Time

_____ Date

Distance

Pace

Route

Running Buddies :

Notes :

You are :
BRAVER than
you believe
STONGER than
you seem
FASTER than
you Think.

Run ∘ Stretch ∘ Breath ∘ Sweat ∘ Drink ∘ Relax ∘ Live

YOU ARE :
BRAVER than
you believe
STONGER than
you seem
FASTER than
you Think.

Run ∘ Stretch ∘ Breath
Sweat ∘ Drink ∘ Relax ∘ Live

Time

_____ Date

Distance

Pace

Route

Running Buddies :

Notes :

You are :
BRAVER than
    you believe
Stonger than
    you seem
Faster than
    you Think.

Run ∘ Stretch ∘ Breath ∘ Sweat ∘ Drink ∘ Relax ∘ Live

you are :
BRAVER than
     you believe
STONGER than
     you seem
FASTER than
     you Think.

Run ○ Stretch ○ Breath
Sweat ○ Drink ○ Relax ○ Live

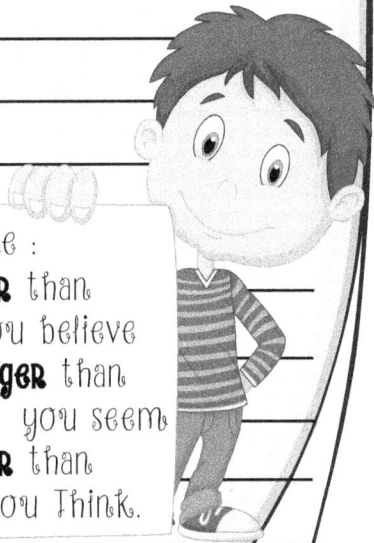

Time

_____ Date

Distance

Pace

Route

Running Buddies :

Notes :

You are :
BRAVER than
    you believe
STONGER than
    you seem
FASTER than
    you Think.

Run ∘ Stretch ∘ Breath ∘ Sweat ∘ Drink ∘ Relax ∘ Live

You are :
BRAVER than
you believe
STONGER than
you seem
FASTER than
you Think.

Run ∘ Stretch ∘ Breath
Sweat ∘ Drink ∘ Relax ∘ Live

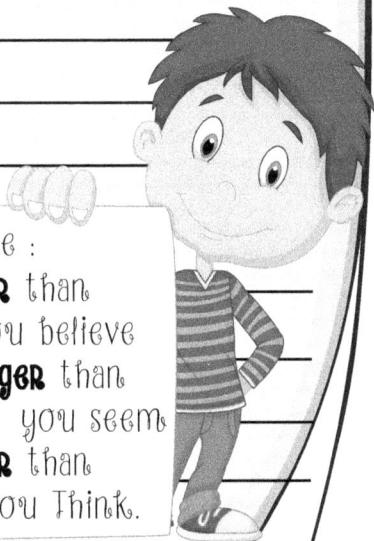